T0061157

Working
Hand in Hand

PATHFINDER EDITION

By Diane G. Silver

CONTENTS

Changing the Tide for Turtles

What is seven feet long, dives 3,000 feet into the sea, and weighs nearly 2,000 pounds? A leatherback turtle! These giant reptiles are in danger. Can anyone save them?

José Urteaga (UHR-TAY-AH-GAH) first saw baby sea turtles when he was a child. Standing on a sandy beach in Nicaragua, he watched wide-eyed as hundreds of newly hatched turtles crawled out of the sand. In the dark of night, they made a run across the beach to the salty sea.

Today, fewer sea turtles than ever are racing toward the waves. Turtles are in danger of dying out. Today, every species of sea turtle in Nicaragua is endangered.

José Urteaga, a marine biologist and a National Geographic Emerging Explorer, wants to save the turtles. He still remembers his first moment with sea turtles. He knows that sea turtles are important to both the environment and to the people of Nicaragua.

2

By Diane G. Silver

Turtle Defender. *José Urteaga finds ways to protect endangered sea turtles in Nicaragua.*

U.S.

S. AMERICA

Nicaragua

For hundreds of years, turtle eggs have been a source of food for people living in Central America. Eating the eggs is part of the culture, or way of life. Selling turtle eggs is also a way to earn money for the people living near turtle nesting beaches.

Urteaga understands the need to conserve, or protect, both turtles and the economy. So he is using science and creativity to find ways to help the turtles and his fellow Nicaraguans. Urteaga explains, "I don't just work with turtles; I work with people."

3

Saving the Leatherbacks

Leatherback sea turtles are the biggest sea turtles on Earth. Leatherbacks are one of the five endangered species of turtles that nest, or lay their eggs, on Nicaragua's sandy beaches. These gentle giants have wandered Earth for more than 100 million years.

In 2002, when José Urteaga began his work in Nicaragua with the organization Fauna & Flora International, the amazing leatherbacks were dying out. But why? Urteaga discovered that poaching was a big part of the answer. Poaching is catching or hunting animals that the law does not allow.

People hunt turtles for their meat. People also hunt for turtle eggs. Turtle eggs are an important food for many Nicaraguans. Many people believe turtle eggs are healthier than eggs from chickens. And Nicaraguans like the way turtle eggs taste, too. People have been selling turtle eggs for centuries.

By 2002, almost every leatherback turtle egg on Nicaragua's Pacific coast had been poached. The number of female leatherbacks laying eggs had dropped about 90 percent. At one point, Urteaga counted only 22 nests. Sadly, he saw that these amazing creatures were going to die out if things didn't change.

Urteaga also learned that some people living near nesting beaches were gathering eggs and selling them. And he understood why. Selling eggs is an important **business** in some seaside communities. Some of the people selling turtle eggs were living on less than one dollar a day. People could **earn** $5.00 by selling just one dozen turtle eggs.

Empty Nest. People collect turtle eggs from beaches to sell.

Traditional Food. Turtle meat has been a source of food for hundreds of years.

The people in beach communities had few other ways, if any, to make money. So selling turtle eggs was important for their survival. But the **poachers** would lose this **income** if the turtles died out. How could people maintain the turtle populations and maintain their income, too?

Protect the Eggs

José Urteaga knew that without turtle eggs, there could be no turtles. So what should he do? Protect the eggs.

Urteaga set up patrols, day and night, on an important leatherback nesting beach. These patrols watch for the half-ton females to drag themselves out of the rolling sea. The patrols then guard the mother turtles as they crawl across the sand to their nesting ground.

As a female prepares to lay her eggs, Urteaga's patrol stands nearby. After the turtle has dug its nest, the patrol slips a plastic bag into the bottom of the nest, so they can capture the prized eggs. They then carefully carry the eggs to a hatchery. Here the eggs are kept warm until the babies hatch, or break out of their shells. On a dark night, the patrol releases the hatchlings into the cool ocean waters.

More Issues for Turtles

Urteaga found more reasons for the disappearing turtles. Early in the 21st century, shark fishing became a big business. The nets used to catch the sharks also catch turtles. Often, the trapped turtles die.

The destruction of beaches where sea turtles lay their eggs added to the problem. So did people who built on beaches that turtles use for their nests. Also, tourists often cause damage to nesting grounds.

Climate change also affects the turtles. Urteaga explains that leatherbacks in the Pacific Ocean are smaller than leatherbacks in other oceans. Pacific leatherbacks also lay fewer eggs. The cause may be changes in the water temperature.

Points of View

Urteaga recognizes that guarding nests is not enough to save the turtles. He explains, "We can't only look at this from the turtle's point of view. We must also see the human side."

So Urteaga works with the people who live near nesting beaches to find new ways for them to earn money. He has taught people to be farmers or beekeepers instead. People who fish for sharks have learned to put turtles trapped in nets back into the water.

Urteaga also believes that by getting to know turtles, people will become their protectors. To build knowledge, children and their families attend "Day of the Turtle" festivals. Urteaga wants children to see real turtles— and be as excited about the amazing reptiles as he was as a child.

Sea Turtle Life Cycle

In the Sand
A baby turtle's life begins two feet beneath the sand on an ocean beach. Female sea turtles lay their eggs in nests that they dig.

Digging Out
Weeks later, baby turtles—or hatchlings—break out of their shells. They dig their way up, up, up and out of the nest.

Into the Water
The tiny hatchlings scurry across the sand to the water. They are trying to avoid hungry birds and crabs that want to eat them.

In the Open Sea
The babies that reach the water safely spend years in the sea. Ninety percent of a sea turtle's life is spent at sea.

Back to the Land
After 30 years at sea, female sea turtles leave the water to lay their eggs. Most travel long distances to make their way to the same sandy beach year after year.

Night Patrol. *Urteaga and his team protect a leatherback turtle as it digs a nest.*

From Poachers to Protectors

Over the last ten years, Urteaga has changed the lives of both the turtles and fellow Nicaraguans. By 2010, 90 percent of leatherback nests at three beaches were protected from poachers. And the team had released over 34,000 turtle hatchlings, or babies, into the sea.

Urteaga set up patrols on other beaches, too. Some of these beaches are where olive ridley and hawksbill sea turtles nest. By 2010, about 50 percent of the nesting hawksbill turtles were also protected.

More than 80 members of the community are working with Urteaga to save the turtles. Some poachers have become protectors. Some people work in the hatcheries where the baby turtles hatch from their eggs.

Because of education, more Nicaraguans understand the need to protect the amazing turtles. The people want to earn a living in ways that do not endanger the giants of the sea.

Urteaga does not congratulate himself for the progress. He says, "I would never say that the project's achievements are ours alone." Urteaga points out that people in the communities, organizations, and businesses all have worked together to help conserve the sea turtles.

Determined to Succeed

Today sea turtles are a little bit safer. Though still endangered, their numbers are no longer dropping. People in seaside communities are taking pride in their beaches and the sea turtles that live among them.

Still, there is work to do. Urteaga wants more community leaders to get involved in turtle conservation. He also stresses the need to keep giving people good ways to earn money.

José Urteaga knows he must continue his work with the turtles and the communities. He explains, "We haven't won the war. It may take the rest of my lifetime, but we are determined to succeed."

Wordwise

business: activity that earns money by making goods or providing a service

earn: to receive money for work you do

economy: the system for organizing money and businesses

income: the money that you earn or receive

poacher: person who catches or hunts animals when it is against the law

Solutions for Success

José Urteaga is a creative problem solver. He gathers facts and tackles problems from many sides. Read the facts and Urteaga's three strategies. Which strategy is the best? You decide.

The Facts

- Sea turtles in Nicaragua are dying out. The turtles and their eggs must be protected. But many people sell turtle meat or turtle eggs for a living.

- Nicaraguans have been eating the tasty and nutritious turtle eggs and meat for hundeds of years. The eggs and meat have healthy protein in them.

- Fishing with nets traps sea turtles along with fish. Often the turtles die.

Turtle hatchling

Circle hooks

Strategy A
Create new jobs!

Urteaga offers local people new ways to earn money. Some people get jobs on beach patrols. Some people help out in hatcheries. Other people learn organic farming or how to raise bees. Some people act as tour guides. Some women make purses out of recycled plastic bags.

Strategy B
Spread the word!

Urteaga wanted to make people in Nicaragua aware of the troubles that sea turtles face. So he sent his message through music. Rock stars gave concerts. Singers told their audiences, "I don't eat turtle eggs." The message reached over a million people.

Strategy C
Teach new fishing techniques!

Urteaga's team teaches people who fish with nets new skills. These people learn how to return turtles to the sea that get caught by accident in the nets. They also find out about a special circle-shaped fishing hook. It is less harmful to the swimming turtles.

TEAM Turtle

Five of the seven endangered species of sea turtles on Earth live in waters off Nicaragua's coast. Find out what makes each one special.

Leatherback Turtle

- **Claim to Fame:** oldest and largest sea turtle on Earth
- **Reason for Its Name:** Its shell feels like leather.
- **Size:** 4–7 feet (120–213 centimeters) long
- **Weight:** 440–2000 pounds (200–900 kilograms)
- **Food:** jellyfish
- **Fun Fact:** can stay underwater for up to 85 minutes

Olive Ridley Turtle

- **Claim to Fame:** Thousands nest on the beach at the same time.
- **Reason for Its Name:** olive green shell
- **Size:** 2–2.5 feet (61–76 centimeters) long
- **Weight:** 77–100 pounds (35–45 kilograms)
- **Food:** shellfish
- **Fun Fact:** sometimes has an extra claw on its front flippers

Green Sea Turtle

- **Claim to Fame:** only plant-eating adult sea turtle
- **Reason for Its Name:** The layer of fat under its shell is green.
- **Size:** 3–4 feet (91–120 centimeters) long
- **Weight:** 240–700 pounds (110–317 kilograms)
- **Food:** sea grass and algae
- **Fun Fact:** has a single pair of scales in front of its eyes

Loggerhead Turtle

- **Claim to Fame:** powerful jaw
- **Reason for Its Name:** its very large head
- **Size:** 2.5–3 feet (76–91 centimeters) long
- **Weight:** 155–375 pounds (70–170 kilograms)
- **Food:** shellfish
- **Fun Fact:** Its shell is heart-shaped.

Hawksbill Sea Turtle

- **Claim to Fame:** very colorful shell
- **Reason for Its Name:** Its beak is shaped like the beak of a hawk.
- **Size:** 2–3.75 feet (61–114 centimeters) long
- **Weight:** 100–150 pounds (45–68 kilograms)
- **Food:** sponges, anemones, squid, shrimp
- **Fun Fact:** uses beak to peck food out of tiny spaces in coral reefs

Saving Elephants
One Village at a Time

Could the largest land animal on Earth, the elephant, disappear forever? Impossible, right? But it almost happened in one part of Africa. Meet the man called "Hammer" who helped elephants—and his people, too.

AFRICA

Zambia

There are two words you would probably never hear Hammer say: "No way!" No matter what problem Hammer faces, he says, "We can do this."

A Man Called "Hammer"

Hammer's full name is Hammerskjoeld (HOM-ur-shold) Simwinga. He was born in Zambia, Africa. Hammer can speak seven local languages. He studied farming, and he has managed big farms. He has also helped people learn how to grow gardens.

With his knowledge of the land and its people, Hammer was just the right person to tackle a problem in North Luangwa National Park. Poachers were killing the elephants in the park to sell the meat and tusks. Elephant tusks are made of valuable ivory. Ivory is used to make things such as jewelry and piano keys. People pay a lot for ivory.

Before poaching began, 17,000 elephants roamed the park. By 1994, only about 1,300 elephants were left.

The villagers living around the park were very poor. Some earned money by working for the poachers. Hammer says, "The whole community was involved." Soon those jobs would disappear along with the elephants.

In 1994, Hammer joined Mark and Delia Owens's conservation project which was helping both the elephants and the villagers. He explains, "My role was to help local people come up with something that would really support them."

One Village at a Time

Hammer knew that if he could teach villagers new ways to earn money, they would stop working for poachers. Hammer put his knowledge to work. He figured out ways each village could earn its living. His strategies help the people, the elephants, and the land.

Hammer and his team gave some villages sunflower seeds to plant. For many years, the villagers had used sunflower oil for cooking. But the oil cost a lot of money. By growing sunflowers, villagers could make their own oil. And they could sell their sunflower oil, too.

Other communities began to raise bees. The villagers eat honey the bees make. They also sell honey to earn money.

Some villagers became fish farmers. Hammer and his team taught people how to raise fish in special ponds. Then people had fish to eat and fish to sell.

Hammer's many different solutions worked. In 64 villages, people stopped helping poachers.

Hope for the Future

In the villages today, "poaching is a thing of the past," Hammer exclaims. So far, he has helped more than 35,000 people. And with new job skills, Hammer explains, the villagers have regained "their joy of life." One villager says, "I now feel hopeful about my future."

Hammer's project also helped the elephants. The number of elephants in the park is growing. And more than 50 other species of animals have come back to the park.

Hammer believes that life in Africa depends on protecting the environment. He says, "If we wipe it out, we wipe out our future." With people like Hammer working for change, we all have a good chance for that future.

Finding Solutions. *Hammer teaches villagers new ways to earn money.*

SOLUTIONS
FOR THE FUTURE

Find out how people can protect nature for the future. Then answer these questions.

1 What is José Urteaga doing to improve things for both turtles and people in Nicaragua?

2 What opinion does the author have of José Urteaga's work? How do you feel about it?

3 Which strategy on page 7 is best? Why do you think so?

4 What problems did Hammer tackle in North Luangwa National Park? How did he solve them?

5 How are José Urteaga and Hammer Simwinga similar? How are they different?